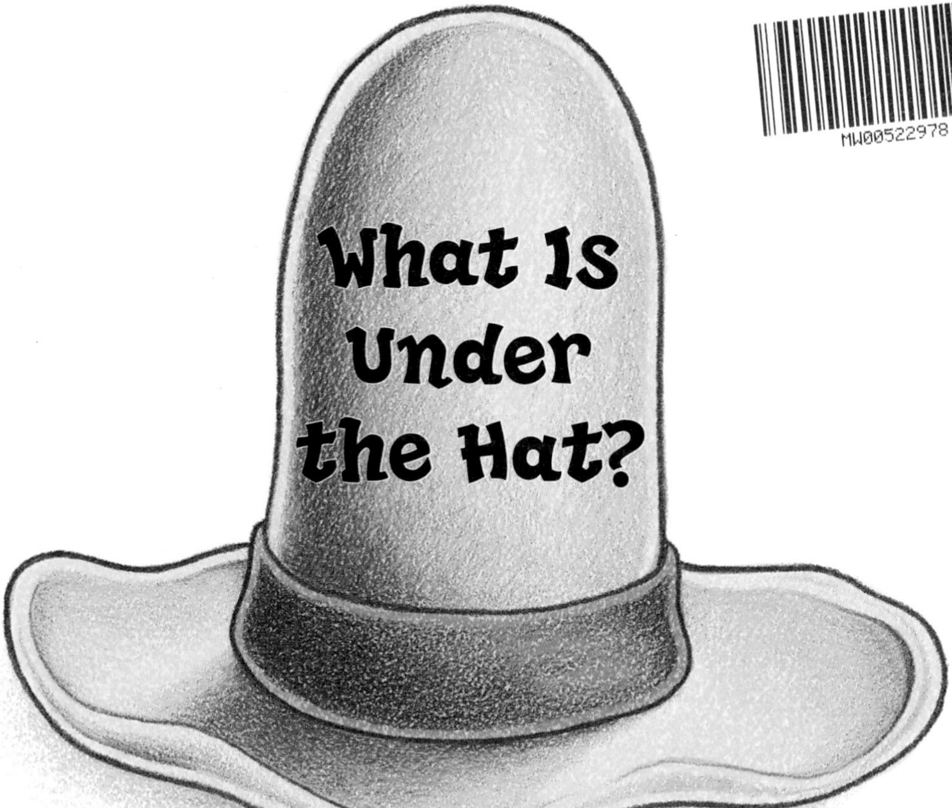

What Is Under the Hat?

Written by Judy Nayer

Illustrated by Gregg Valley

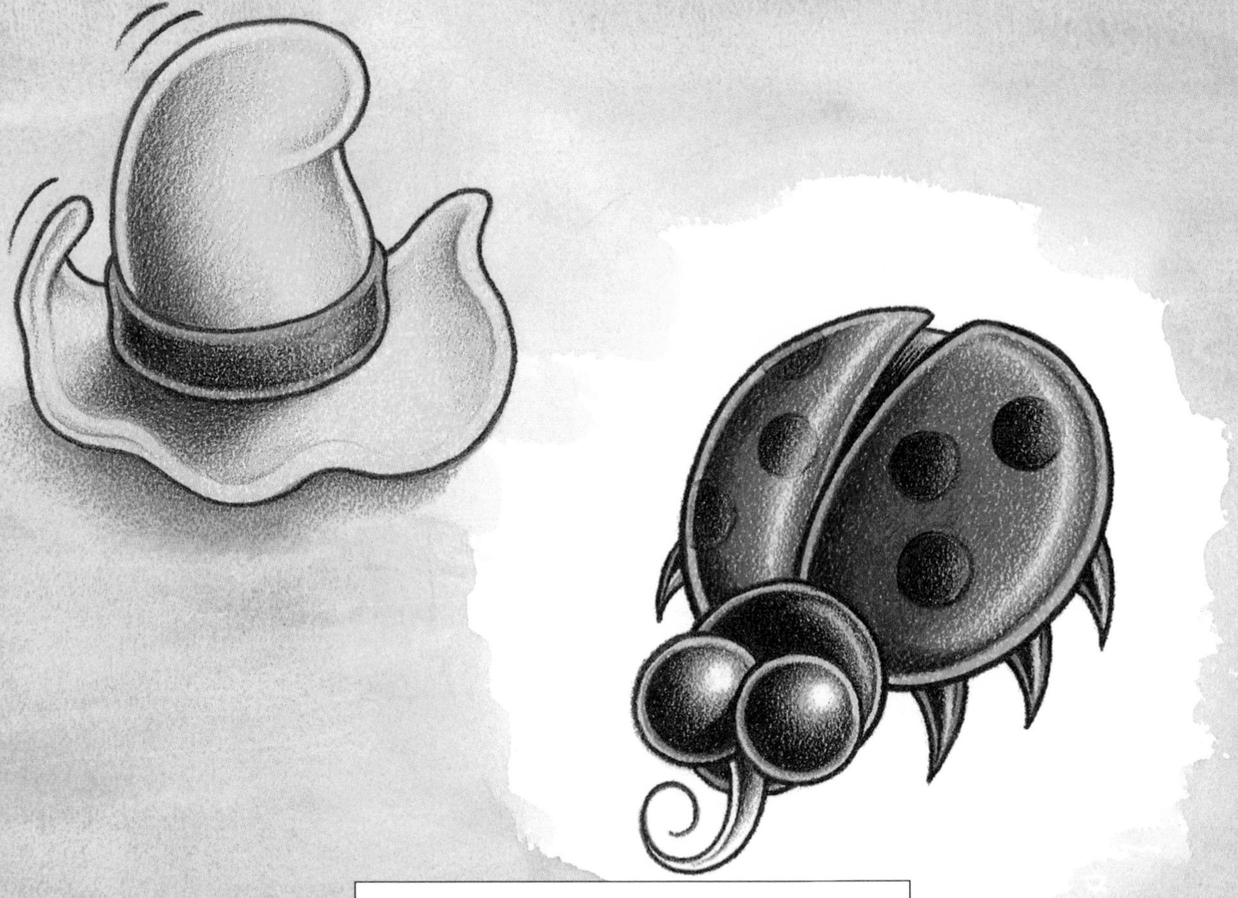

Is it a bug?

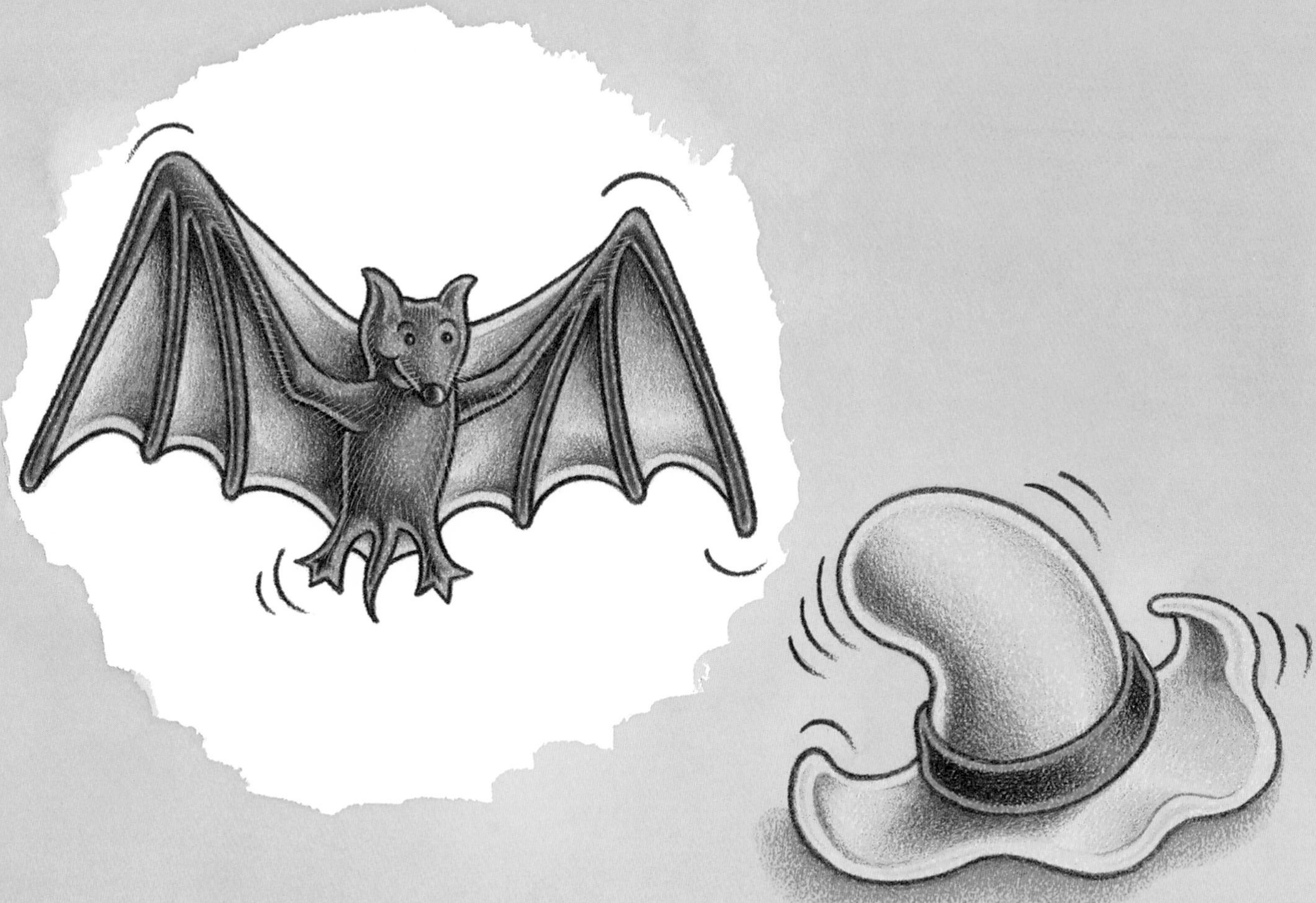

Is it a bat?

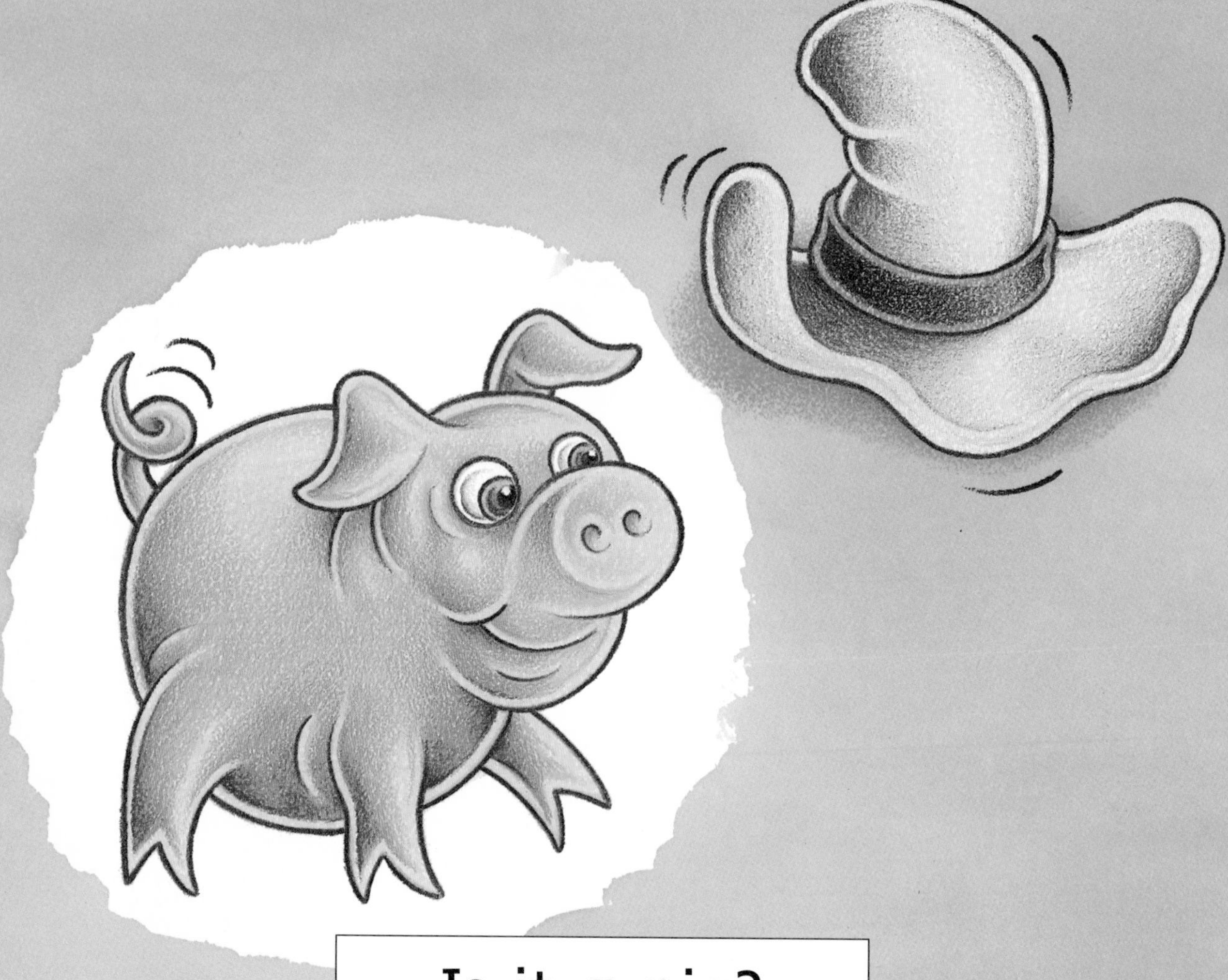

Is it a pig?

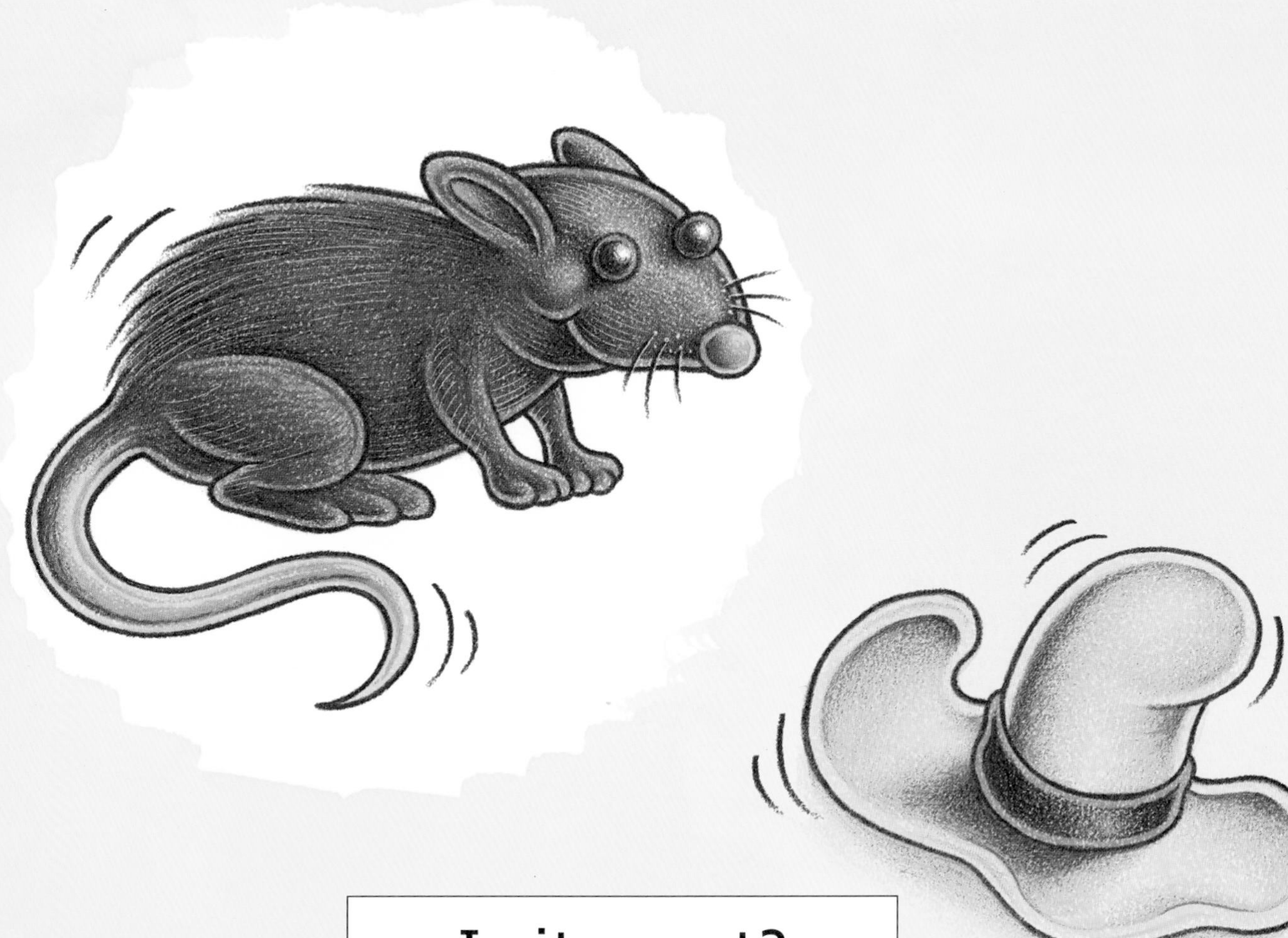

Is it a rat?

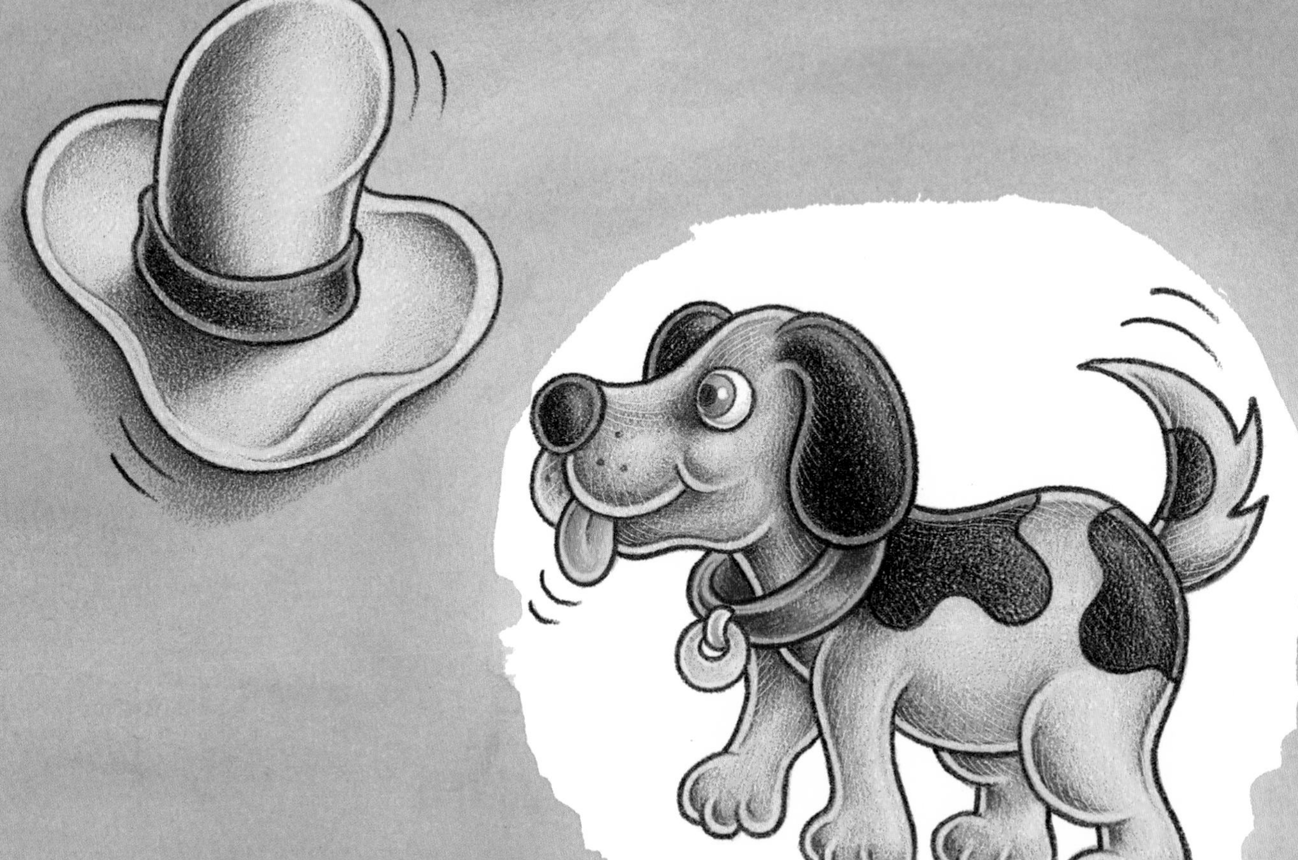

Is it a dog?

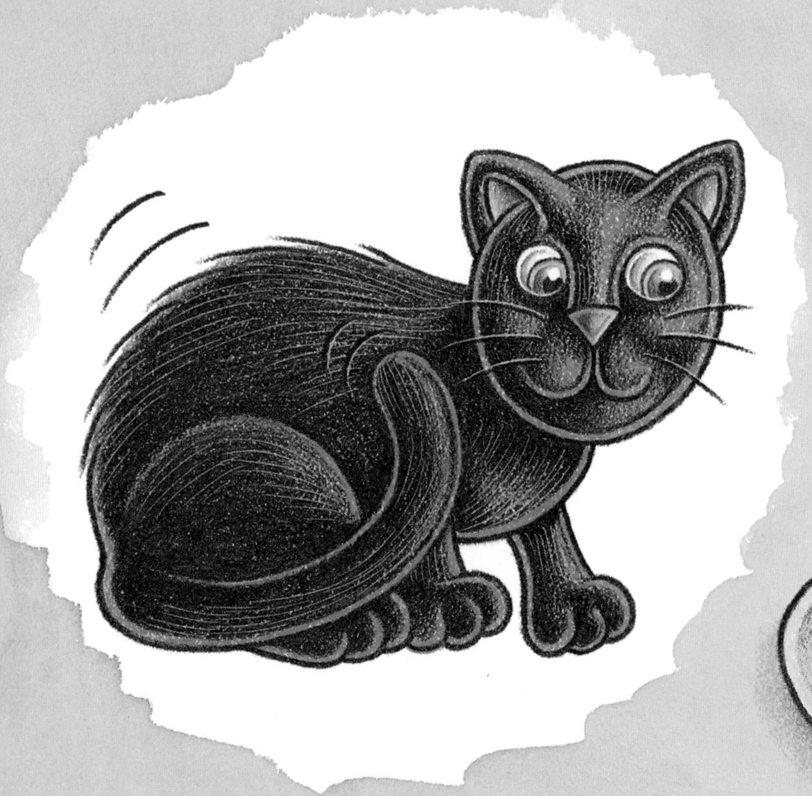

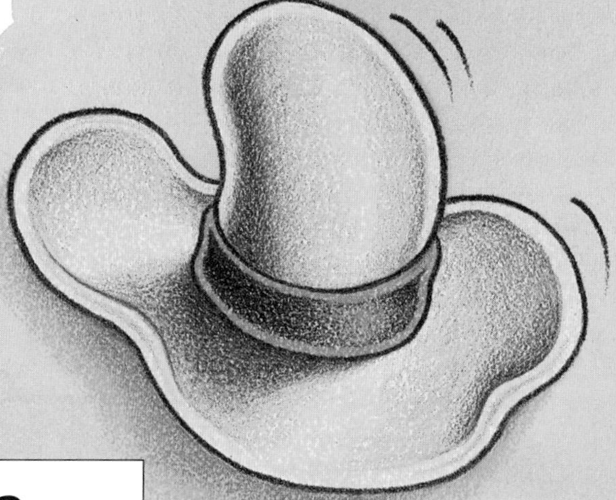

Is it a cat?

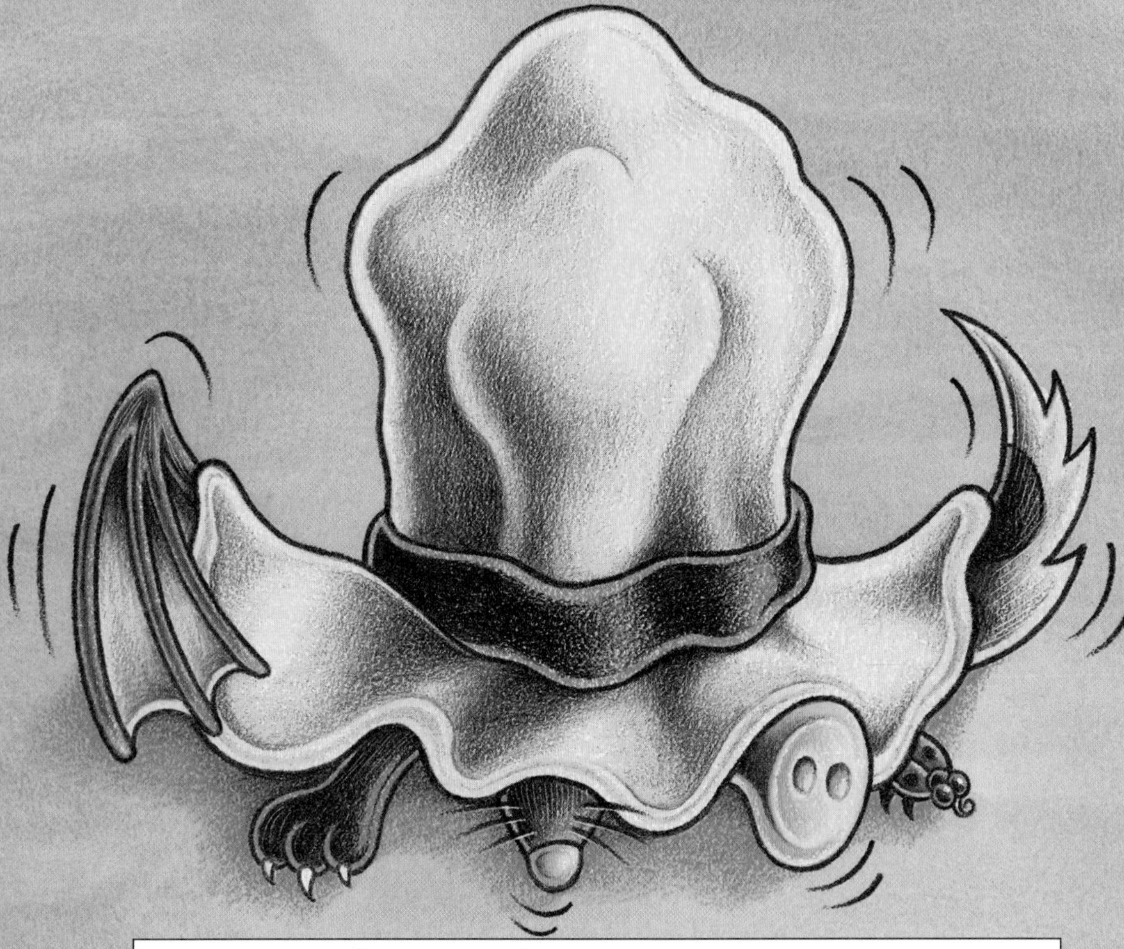

What is under the hat?